RUNNING FOR MENTAL HEALTH: A HOW-TO GUIDE

By Kjersti Nelson

For Liesl, Maxwell, Henry, and Greg who support me through thick and thin, and inspire me every single day.

And to my parents, brothers and sisters who were my original running partners and continue to be my sounding boards for all things running.

Illustrated by Emily Doliner

© 2019 by Kjersti Nelson. All rights reserved.

An Introduction:
THE BENEFITS OF RUNNING FOR MENTAL HEALTH

Running is a great tool for regulating mood and sustaining a sense of well-being. It is a coping skill for dealing with life's ebbs and flows. All people's mental health benefits from running.

What is it about running that improves mental health?

RUNNING PROMOTES MOOD STABILITY

At the bare bones, running causes chemical and hormonal changes in the body that promote mood stability. The parts of the brain that are activated during a run also contribute to a sense of well-being and stable mood.

RUNNING BUILDS CONFIDENCE

The sense of achievement that comes from a single run, a race, and a running habit promote feelings of self-esteem, self-efficacy, accomplishment, and confidence. However, not every run is ideal, and not every training season is either. Running mirrors the ebbs and flows of life and promotes a sense of resilience---I can do hard things! I can withstand difficulty! I will make it through!!

RUNNING IS MOMENTUM FOR CHANGE

In life, getting started on anything is often the hardest part. Running reflects this aspect of life. It is a literal step forward; motion that creates emotion; movement in a forward direction.

RUNNING CALMS A BUSY MIND

Lastly, running provides a plethora of opportunities to meditate, socialize, be in nature, and practice gratitude.

To expand a little on these concepts...

Routine running literally transforms the brain. The hippocampus (responsible for memory), prefrontal cortex (responsible for logic and cognition), and amygdala (responsible for emotion) are activated by running. The activation of these parts of the brain often help a person to feel more awake, aware, creative, and emotionally self-attuned. Studies have shown that runners have more brain derived neurotropic factor (BDNF) present in these parts of the brain too, which has been linked to feelings of well-being and lower levels of depression.

These changes in the brain lead to creative out-of-the-box ways of thinking, which (when recognized and acted on) can be opportunities for finding new meaning in experiences and personal "stories", as well as discovering unique solutions to life's problems, or even just an opportunity to experience a delightful respite from the usual thought patterns.

Adding to that, runners can expect to have increased neurotransmitters present in the brain in the long-term, including norepinephrine, serotonin, and dopamine. These neurotransmitters are the same chemicals that are often found in antidepressants and work to promote feelings of well-being, regulate mood, and sharpen focus. Interestingly, runners are less likely to suffer from insomnia, and experience deeper sleep, which also contributes to a sharper mind and mood stabilization.

Hormonally, runners experience a decrease in cortisol, a hormone commonly known for increasing stress and anxiety. And as any runner can tell you, running can provide a cathartic release from daily stress and anxiety.

The caveat, you do have to make running a routine to benefit in the long-term. Although the famous "runner's high" and the "cathartic release" results from these same neurochemicals and hormonal changes, these are fleeting experiences. A stable mood, on the other hand, can only be sustained through the long-term habit of running.

Self-esteem and confidence are some of the first changes a new runner may experience. To go from enduring a 1-mile walk to conquering a 1-mile run is a big accomplishment. No one can do it for you. Only by persistence and hard work can you get there, so when you do, your self-esteem and confidence get a boost. This translates to how you perceive other obstacles in your life, as your sense of self-efficacy is enhanced. Not to mention the confidence gained from overall improved physical health like better heart health, increased stamina, and stronger muscles and bones. As your running improves, you'll begin to take pride in how you care for yourself—through running—and that is the greatest confidence boost of all.

Along the way, you'll develop resilience. Once routine and physical stamina are established, most runs will feel less labored; however, running can still be sluggish and downright challenging at times. On those days your capacity for resilience grows. You do it anyway, knowing that when it's difficult you grow the most. Your attitude becomes, "I can do hard things!"

Runners are often set up for success based on making short-term and long-term goals. Initially you may work for a week or few to run your very first mile. When that goal is achieved you can then visualize how you might reach the next bigger goal, 2 miles and on and on. Running teaches us how to plan and work in manageable steps to reach our goals. Those small steps provide momentum for change, and every milestone feels rewarding.

Lastly, there are other mental health benefits to running that can be added in. Running is a great time to socialize or a great time to ponder and process alone. Running can be used as a form of meditation, or can be a rambunctious joyful adventure. If running outside, the benefits of being in nature are an added sense of calm and a deepened sense of gratitude as the feeling of awe sets in.

GETTING STARTED

Now you know **the why** to running for your mental health. Here is **the how**.

Make a Plan. Be realistic. If you are brand new to running, you'll want to choose 2-4 days per week to run 15 minutes or more. Grow your distance gradually. Include walking in that plan for the first few weeks. (See sample plans)

Write Down Your Goals and Tell Someone. Is your run goal to get in shape? To complete a 5k? 10k? ½ or Full marathon? Write it down and tell someone. Statistically you're more likely to reach your goals if you do.

What is your **mental health goal** associated with running? To run off steam? To cope with depressive symptoms? To be your best self? To find respite from life's stressors? To improve a relationship? To be more in touch with your feelings and felt senses? Whether one of these goals or another, running is a great way to improve mental health.

Make Time. Training takes time. To reach your goal you may have to commit to weeks or months or even years. Will you have to get up early in the morning before work? Head to the gym after dinner? Go for a jog on your lunch break? Fitting your runs into your routine is how they become routine. At first finding the motivation to just go will be difficult. The more you commit to going at a certain time the more likely you'll establish a habit of running, and the habit facilitates the motivation.

Commit. Running is not always comfortable, especially in the beginning when you're growing your capacity for endurance and strength. It can be hard. Know that there is light at the end of the tunnel, and that through commitment you'll one day reach that light! It's important to remember that even if you miss a run, all is not lost. Just pick back up where you left off the next day.

Believe in Yourself. Be your own best cheerleader. Tell yourself, "I can do hard things"! Then you will. Make a list of affirmations that mean something to you. Repeat them to yourself on your run, like a mantra.

Set an intention, or meditate. Any individual run can have a purpose outside of the physical running. Before you set out to run reflect for a moment on what you'd like to gain. Do you want to hone in on an intention? Intentions are a sort of mental focus. Examples of intentions could be reflecting on gratitude, or experiencing peace, finding clarity, or relaxing your mind. You might choose a mantra as an intention. Or meditate on your breath and movement. You might want to reflect on an experience or a relationship. Perhaps you want to be outside in nature experiencing your senses, or allowing your mind to wander to have creative outlet.

Journal. Like with dreams, the dynamic and creative thoughts you have while on a run tend to be fleeting. If you don't write it down, soon those moments of clarity, creativity, and reminiscence slip away. Get in the habit of taking notes about your run, your feelings, and your thoughts. Not only does journaling help you retain the feelings and thoughts you had on the run, they become a tangible record of your progress as well as useful information to consider in future plans as you grow and change.

Find a Friend. One of the greatest joys of running is finding a friend to join in the journey. Not necessarily for every single run. Those solo runs can be quite sacred. BUT, the camaraderie, support, and joy of running-friendships can last a lifetime.

YOUR RUN PLAN

Now you have **the why** and **the how**. Here is **the do**.

1. What is your run goal?
2. What is your mental health goal?
3. Choose how you will incorporate your mental health goal into any given run (these will vary most runs):
   - ☐ Running meditation
   - ☐ Set an intention to focus your thoughts.
   - ☐ Sensory run (eliminate devices/apps, run how you feel, notice all your senses and surroundings.
   - ☐ Choose a question/scenario you want to evaluate in your mind.
   - ☐ Choose a feeling/relationship you want to evaluate in your mind.
   - ☐ Run with a friend and socialize.
   - ☐ Let your mind wander, daydream, be creative.
   - ☐ Journal after your run to remember the aha moments, the intense feelings, and creative places your mind went.
   - ☐ Run for running's sake. No goal is a goal. You will benefit mentally just by getting out there.
4. How many days can you commit to running per week?
5. List the days you plan to run (consider using one of the training plans provided):
6. What time of day do you plan to run?
7. What will you do to prepare ahead of time to eliminate obstacles to your run commitment?
8. Who can you tell your run goal and run plan for support?
9. Write down some affirmations or mantras that will help you be your own best cheerleader:
10. Contact any friends you'd like to invite along.

Choose the run plan that most suits your circumstances (adjust as needed):

LEARN-TO-RUN PLAN

	MON	TUES	WED	THURS	FRI	SAT	SUN
week 1	2 min jog 2 min walk **Repeat 4 times**		2 min jog 2 min walk **Repeat 4 times**		2 min jog 2 min walk **Repeat 5 times**		
week 2	3 min jog 2 min walk **Repeat 3 times**		3 min jog 2 min walk **Repeat 3 times**		3 min jog 1 min walk **Repeat 5 times**		
week 3	3 min jog 1 min walk **Repeat 4 times**		3 min jog 1 min walk **Repeat 4 times**		3 min jog 1 min walk **Repeat 6 times**		
week 4	5 min jog 2 min walk **Repeat 3 times**		5 min jog 2 min walk **Repeat 3 times**		5 min jog 1 min walk **Repeat 5 times**		
week 5	15 min jog		20 min jog		30 min jog		

BEFORE STARTING ANY NEW EXERCISE ROUTINE, ALWAYS CONSULT WITH YOUR PRIMARY CARE PHYSICIAN. DO NOT DO THESE PROGRAMS IF YOU ARE NOT HEALTHY ENOUGH TO PARTICIPATE.

5K TRAINING PLAN

	MON	TUES	WED	THURS	FRI	SAT	SUN
week 1	10 min jog		15 min jog		20 min jog		
week 2	1½ miles		1½ miles		2 miles		
week 3	2 miles		2 miles		3 miles		
week 4	3 miles		3 miles		3½ miles		
week 5	3 miles		3½ miles		4 miles		

Try adding in 3-6 x 60 second bursts of speed on the Monday runs (weeks 3-5). Take 60 seconds jogging or walking in-between the bursts for recovery)

BEFORE STARTING ANY NEW EXERCISE ROUTINE, ALWAYS CONSULT WITH YOUR PRIMARY CARE PHYSICIAN. DO NOT DO THESE PROGRAMS IF YOU ARE NOT HEALTHY ENOUGH TO PARTICIPATE.

10K TRAINING PLAN

	MON	TUES	WED	THURS	FRI	SAT	SUN
week 1	2 miles		2 miles		3 miles		3 miles
week 2	2 miles		2 miles		3 miles		4 miles
week 3	2 miles		2½ miles		3 miles		4½ miles
week 4	2 miles		3 miles		3 miles		5 miles
week 5	2 miles		3 miles		3 miles		5½ miles
week 6	2 miles		3 miles		3 miles		6.2 miles

Try adding in 3-6 x 60 second bursts of speed on the Wednesday runs. Take 60 seconds jogging or walking in-between the bursts for recovery)

If you are new to running and want to complete a 10k, complete the Learn-to-Run and 5k Training Plan first.

BEFORE STARTING ANY NEW EXERCISE ROUTINE, ALWAYS CONSULT WITH YOUR PRIMARY CARE PHYSICIAN. DO NOT DO THESE PROGRAMS IF YOU ARE NOT HEALTHY ENOUGH TO PARTICIPATE.

MAINTENANCE PLAN

	MON	TUES	WED	THURS	FRI	SAT	SUN
week 1	2 miles		3 miles		4 miles		
week 2	2 miles		3 miles		5 miles		
week 3	2 miles		3 miles		6 miles		
week 4	2 miles		3 miles		4miles		
week 5	2 miles		3 miles		5 miles		

Continue to repeat weeks 1-5

BEFORE STARTING ANY NEW EXERCISE ROUTINE, ALWAYS CONSULT WITH YOUR PRIMARY CARE PHYSICIAN. DO NOT DO THESE PROGRAMS IF YOU ARE NOT HEALTHY ENOUGH TO PARTICIPATE.

DAILY RUNNING PLAN

(a type of maintenance plan)

	MON	TUES	WED	THURS	FRI	SAT	SUN
week 1	1-3 miles	1-3 miles	1-3 miles	1-3 miles	1-3 miles	1-5 miles	Rest
week 2	1-3 miles	1-3 miles	1-3 miles	1-3 miles	1-3 miles	1-5 miles	Rest

Repeat as needed. Don't run every run at a hard pace. 3-5 of the runs should be at a slow, easy pace.

BEFORE STARTING ANY NEW EXERCISE ROUTINE, ALWAYS CONSULT WITH YOUR PRIMARY CARE PHYSICIAN. DO NOT DO THESE PROGRAMS IF YOU ARE NOT HEALTHY ENOUGH TO PARTICIPATE.

NUTRITION, SLEEP & EXERCISE

Running for mental health is a lifestyle commitment. It isn't all just about running. There are two other parts of the puzzle: Nutrition & Sleep.

Nutrition, sleep, and exercise help to level out the chemical reactions and hormonal imbalances happening in your body and brain as well as provide the required respite and recovery needed in the brain and body to function optimally.

There is a saying, "one run may change your day, but many runs will change your life." Another, "One bad meal won't make you fat, AND one good meal won't make you skinny." And finally, "Early to bed and early to rise makes a [wo]man healthy, wealthy, and wise." These three common sentiments touch on the importance of routine in regards to the big three mood regulators. If you can make a habit of healthy eating, consistent quality sleep/rest, and regular exercise you will see improvements in your mood overall.

GENERAL GUIDELINES:

NUTRITION

Eat whole foods and eat all things in moderation. Limit processed foods. Eat mindfully, notice when you are full, notice when you are hungry vs. thirsty, notice how a particular food makes you feel. It's ok to splurge sometimes.

Benefits: Nutrition can level out hormonal imbalances; and impact the brain chemicals serotonin, dopamine, and norepinephrine.

SLEEP

Creating routines at bedtime and getting a full 7-8 hours of sleep at night is recommended for adults. If this is difficult find other ways to "rest the brain and body." Include meditation, doing relaxing activities like reading, listening to calm music, and lounging.

Benefits: Rest reduces cortisol levels (stress hormone), helps keep level serotonin, dopamine, and norepinephrine. Brain and body reparations are made at the cell level while sleeping.

A recommended bedtime routine to encourage deep sleep: As you wind down in the evening lower your lights, drink a warm beverage like milk or chamomile tea, get cozy. In bed try a guided muscle relaxation meditation.

TECHNIQUE:
BREATHING PATTERN FOR RUNNING

Your breathing regulates your entire system. When first learning to run, mastering a functional breathing pattern will make the experience more comfortable and more efficient. I recommend breathing through your mouth, short breaths in, long breaths out. Breathing in this way will help keep your heart rate regulated, and help you avoid "sucking in air," which can cause light-headedness, the runner's cough, and a chest burn.

Breathe through your mouth instead of your nose - it relaxes the jaw, and is more efficient.

TIP:
Try pushing the bottom lip out to forcefully exhale.

Allow your lungs to fully expand by breathing with your diaphragm. Be cautious not to "suck in" air.

.5 L
Average Chest Breath

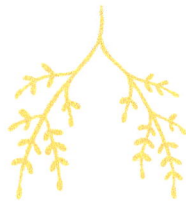

3.6 L
Fully Expanded Stomach Breath

BREATHE WITH YOUR CADENCE

Breathing with cadence helps to control the breath and regulate the heart rate. Make a habit of inhaling on LEFT-RIGHT foot strikes and exhaling on LEFT-RIGHT-LEFT foot strikes. You may have to slow down your pace to practice. Proper breathing technique improves the flow of oxygen to the muscles.

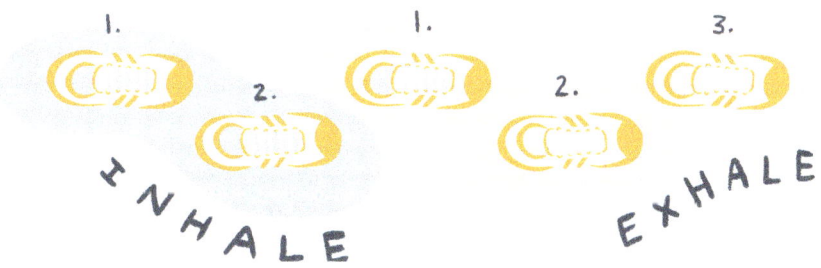

TECHNIQUE:
PROPER RUNNING FORM

Running can feel difficult at times, but it should never feel painful. If you feel pain, stop. Running with proper form facilitates the ease of running and reduces the risk of injury. The below image describes the movement.

TIP: Rather than focusing on every movement, focus on keeping relaxed arm motion. What the arms do, the legs will follow.

HEAD — Level and gazing straight ahead

SHOULDERS — Relaxed and pulled away from ears

HANDS — Loose fists, unclenched

ARMS — Swing naturally front to back, limit crossing the body.

ELBOWS — 90 degree angle

STRIDE ANGLE — Form a 90 degree angle

FEET — Land mid-foot, to heel, then toes push off.

TECHNIQUE:
SHOE BUYING GUIDE

Wearing high quality running shoes, that are fitted to your particular gait, is the number one thing you can do to prevent injury from running. Here's your how-to:

 Consult a fitting specialist in a running store.

② Determine your foot landing type, size and width.

③ Buy one size larger than usual (your feet expand when you run).

④ Try on multiple models, and give each one a test run.

HOW TO DO A RUNNING MEDITATION

Walking and running meditation is not just for stretching our legs. It is a technique as powerful as sitting meditations—and with added benefits! Highlighted here are 3 types of running meditation: The breathing practice, the sensory experience, and mantras.

GENERAL PRINCIPLES FOR RUNNING MEDITATIONS

When running (or walking) keep the head upright and relaxed. Go slowly at your own pace. Remove the idea of judgment as it comes from yourself or others. As you run release muscle tensions which develop in the body. Do not rush, move forward at a gentle pace. Rushing may be a response to discomfort. Consciously let go of that discomfort by releasing any tension in the body.

*Do be aware of your surroundings so that you practice safely.

1. The Breathing Practice: Rhythmic breathing is essential to a fluid running experience. As you meditate, continuously come back to the constant of your breath. Resist grabbing thoughts that rush to mind, let thoughts rise and fall, maintaining a non-judgmental attitude. Find a breath count that feels good to you. Try one short breath count in and 2-3 long breath counts out. Breathe in gently, breathe out forcefully through the mouth. Find a rhythm that works for you. Try matching the rhythm of your breath to your cadence (foot strike), and let your entire movement and breath become in-sync. This practice is similar to a traditional sitting meditation where at any moment you can refocus to your breath, and thoughts are let go with a judgment free attitude.

2. The Sensory Experience: This type of meditation is about mindfully attuning to all 5 senses. As each foot lands on the ground, consciously note how it feels. Be alert to the intention to lift, move, or place your feet. Allow concentration on subtle sensations. Notice the texture of the ground, the temperature, the weight of your body shifting, vibrations, sounds, and smells. Engage all the senses: touch, sight, taste, sound, and smell. As thoughts or memories emerge, note them then let them go. Honor your body and the "messages" it gives about exploring your limits and when to stop. To really tune in try running without music or apps blasting in your ears, maybe don't even pay attention to your watch.

3. Mantras: Mantras are short phrases or words that are repeated for meditative or motivational purposes. Mantras help to build mental-strength and resilience as you repeat something positive to yourself. A mantra can also be used to moderate the breath by sharing a rhythm-beat with cadence (the beat of your foot strike). Like the beat to lyrics in a song, mantras can match the cadence-beat.

SAMPLE RUNNING MANTRAS:

"I can do hard things"

"May I be filled with loving-kindness."

"I can. I will."

"This is what growth feels like."

"Love in. Hate out."

"Light and fast."

"Breathe in, breathe out."

"Relax and breathe."

These meditation practices will help to coordinate body, breath, and mind leaving the runner with a deeper sense of tranquility.

MENTAL HEALTH RUNNING JOURNAL

DAY	DISTANCE & TIME	FEELINGS BEFORE	FEELINGS DURING	FEELINGS AFTER	NOTES

MENTAL HEALTH RUNNING JOURNAL (CONTINUED)

DAY	DISTANCE & TIME	FEELINGS BEFORE	FEELINGS DURING	FEELINGS AFTER	NOTES

JOURNAL

A place to record thoughts, emotions, memories, ideas, and "aha" moments that occurred to you while running.

REFERENCES

Douglas, Scott (2018) Running Is My Therapy: relieve stress and anxiety, fight depression, ditch bad habits, and live happier. New York, NY. The Experiment, LLC.

Havey, Mackenzie (2018) Mindful Running: how meditative running can improve performance and make you a happier, more fulfilled person. Bloomsbury.

Hutchinson, Alex (2018). Endure: mind, body, and the curiously elastic limits of human performance. Harper Collins.

Kastor, Deena & Hamilton, Michelle (2018) Let Your Mind Run: a memoir of thinking my way to victory. New York. Crown Archetype, Penguin Random House.

Mipham, Sakyong (2012). Running with the Mind of Meditation: lessons for training body and mind. New York, NY. Random House.

North American Academy for Sports Fitness Professionals, Marathon Coach Distance Program, North American Edition, Second Edition (2015). Mississauga, ON. Danlyn Group Services Inc.

Pullen, William (2017). Running with Mindfulness: dynamic running therapy (DRT) to improve low-mood, anxiety, stress, and depression. New York, NY. Penguin Random House.

Shapiro, Shauna (2010). Minfulness-Based Stress Reduction Workbook for CPSY 385, Santa Clara University Circa 2010

www.ingramcontent.com/pod-product-compliance
Lightning Source LLC
LaVergne TN
LVHW070837080426
835510LV00026B/3430